Strangers Can Hurt

Written By
Joel M. Caplan

Graphic Design By
Joel M. Caplan &
Oranit Dror-Caplan

Summary: Teaches children that strangers are anyone that they do not know.
Some strangers may be safe, but children should always be cautious of new people
until their parent or other guardian instructs them otherwise.

For My Children.
I Love You Thiiiiiiiiiiiiiiiiiiiiiiiiiiiiiiiiiis Much!

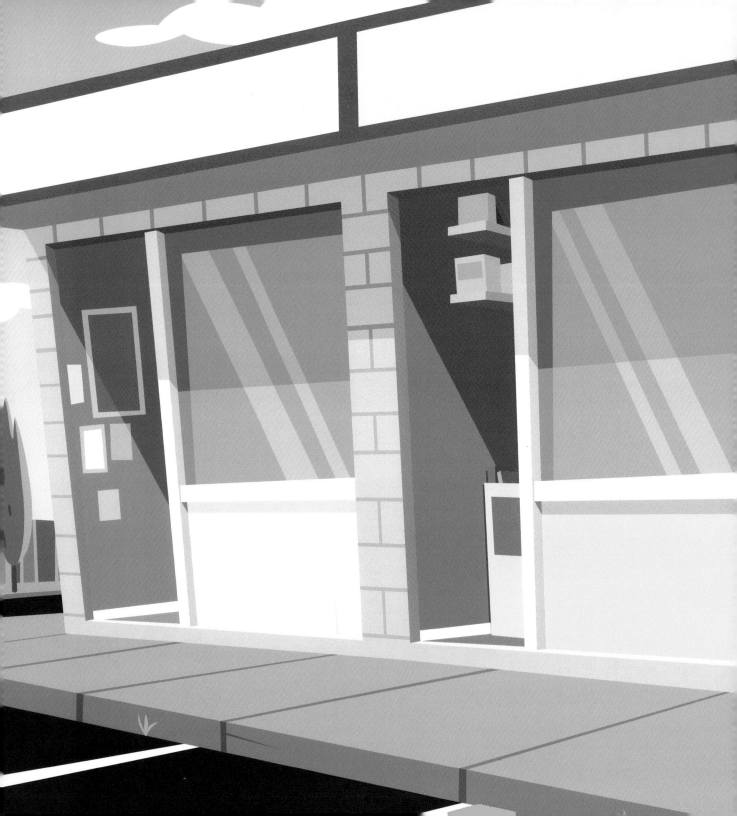

About the Author

Joel M. Caplan has a PhD in Social Welfare from the University of Pennsylvania. He is Assistant Professor at Rutgers University School of Criminal Justice and Associate Director of the Rutgers Center on Public Security. Joel has past professional experience as a police officer and is now an internationally recognized scholar of crime risk analysis and victimization. He is also a proud father.

Additional Safety Tips

Select a code word with your child in case of an emergency. If anyone unexpectedly tells your child to come with them, teach your child to ask for the code word. Make the word easy to remember but also meaningful to your family so other people cannot figure it out.

Teach your child how to use a telephone and to call the police for help.
Call 911, where available.

At the earliest age, teach your child his/her full name, address, and telephone number(s).

Avoid putting clothing or other items on your child that publicly display his/her name.

When the doorbell rings or someone knocks at home, teach children to always ask a parent before opening the door.

If you are out with your child and get separated, teach your child to stay where he/she is and let the parent find him/her. Or when in a store, teach your child to immediately go to the cashier or security guard for help.

One of the most important tools for police to use when locating a missing child is a recent head–and–shoulders, good–quality, photograph. Update photos every 6 months.

CPSIA information can be obtained at www.ICGtesting.com
Printed in the USA
LVIW01n1217100316
478614LV00004B/18